Honestly, RED RIDING HOOD WAS ROTTEN!

The Story of LITTLE RED RIDING HOOD as Told by THE WOLF

by Trisha Speed Shaskan

illustrated by Gerald Guerlais

PICTURE WINDOW BOOKS
a capstone imprint

Special thanks to our adviser, Terry Flaherty, PhD, Professor of English,
Minnesota State University, Mankato, for his expertise.

⁓·ↄ♌ᕤ✤☽ᕤↄ·⁓

Editor: Jill Kalz
Designer: Lori Bye
Art Director: Nathan Gassman
Production Specialist: Sarah Bennett
The illustrations in this book were created digitally.

⁓·ↄ♌ᕤ✤☽ᕤↄ·⁓

Picture Window Books
151 Good Counsel Drive
P.O. Box 669
Mankato, MN 56002-0669
877-845-8392
www.capstonepub.com

All books published by Picture Window Books
are manufactured with paper containing at least
10 percent post-consumer waste.

Library of Congress Cataloging-in-Publication Data
Shaskan, Trisha Speed, 1973–
Honestly, Red Riding Hood was rotten! : the story of Little Red Riding
Hood as told by the wolf / written by Trisha Speed Shaskan ; illustrated
by Gerald Guerlais.
p. cm. — (The other side of the story)
Summary: The Big Bad Wolf, who claims to be a vegetarian, tells his
side of the story of Little Red Riding Hood and her granny.
ISBN 978-1-4048-6673-7 (library binding)
ISBN 978-1-4048-7046-8 (paperback)
[1. Fairy tales. 2. Humorous stories.] I. Guerlais, Gerald, ill. II. Title.
PZ8.S3408Ho 2012
[E]—dc22   2011006995

Printed in the United States of America, North Mankato, MN
092011   006340R

Chomp! Chomp! Oh, I'm sorry. I was just finishing my lunch. My name's Wolf—Big Bad Wolf. You may have heard the story of Little Red Riding Hood. About a girl and her granny? Seems everyone has. My tail is different. Did I say *tail*? I meant *tale*.

The cupboards were bare. The freezer too. And I'd eaten every last vegetable and fruit in the garden. **Every one.**

Other wolves might've lunched on little forest critters: chipmunks, bunnies, squirrels. But I'm a vegetarian. That's right; I don't eat meat. Well, I *try* not to. I **LOVE** apples. Honeycrisp, Pink Lady, Golden Delicious ... Any kind, really. But, sadly, it was a long time until apple harvest.

I hadn't eaten in weeks. My stomach growled and howled. It moaned and groaned. It even roared. Then, my nose took over.

Sniff. Sniff. I took a whiff. What was it?

A girl.

Sniff. Sniff. I took a whiff. What was it?

Cake. Butter. In *this* forest? I had to investigate.

And there she was: Little Red Riding Hood. She looked as plump and juicy as a big, sweet APPLE.

Little Red waved her cape. "Isn't it pretty?" she said.

"Yeah," I said.

"Aren't I pretty?" she said.

Was she admiring herself in that puddle?

"With this cape," she said, "I'm even prettier than usual."

Boy, someone sure was full of herself. My stomach growled.

Little Red twirled a strand of hair. "Mother says the cape looks grand with my skin. My skin shines likes pearls."

Or the meat of a ripe apple, I thought, licking my chops.

Remember, I hadn't eaten in weeks.

Time to chomp!

But then Little Red said, "I can't wait until Granny sees how pretty I am today. I'm bringing her cake and butter from my mother."

My stomach howled. TWO meals, I thought: Granny for breakfast, Little Red for lunch (and cake and butter for dessert).

"Where does Granny live?" I asked.

Little Red pointed. "Down there, in the clearing. The brown house."

I knew that house. And I had a plan.

"Let's play a game," I said.

Little Red smiled. "I'm awesome at games."

"I bet you are," I said. "You take this path. I'll take that path. And let's see who arrives at Granny's first."

"I will," she said. "I'm the prettiest *and* the fastest."

"I bet you are," I said.

My stomach moaned. Before it groaned, I ran.
No one knows the forest like I do. I chose the
shorter path.

THIS PATH

THAT PATH

Sniff. Sniff. I took a whiff. What was it?

Apple air freshener?

Tap, tap. I knocked on the door.

"Who's there?" called out a voice.

"Your granddaughter," I squeaked. "I've brought you cake and butter from Mother."

"Door's open," Granny said.

Granny tugged at her nightcap. "Green," she said. "Isn't it pretty?"

Pretty like a Granny Smith apple, I thought.

"Aren't I pretty?" Granny said.

You must've heard the saying "the apple doesn't fall far from the tree"? Well, it's true.

My stomach roared.

"What's that noise?" Granny asked.

Chomp! Chomp!

I *had* to eat her. She was no
McIntosh apple, but not too bad.

I still felt hungry.

Tap, tap. Little Red knocked on the door.

"Who's there?" I called out, crawling into Granny's bed.

"Your granddaughter," Little Red said. "I've brought you cake and butter from Mother."

"Door's open," I said.

Little Red walked in and caught a glimpse of herself in the mirror. "Isn't my cape pretty, Granny?" she said. "Aren't I pretty?"

I clenched my teeth.

"**Granny,**" Little Red said,
"what deep dark eyes I have."

"**Mmmhmm,**" I said,
"the color of apple seeds."

"**Granny,**" she said,
"what perfect ears I have."

"**Mmmhmm,**" I said,
"shaped like sharply cut apple slices."

20

"**Granny,**" she said,
"what pretty red lips I have."

"**Mmmhmm,**" I said, "Red Delicious."

"**Granny,**" she said,
"what lovely skin I have."

Chomp! Chomp!

I ate her up. What can I say? Things look different when you're hungry. She was no Fuji or Crispin apple (in fact, to be honest, she was a bit rotten), but she was better than nothing.

Plus, I got dessert.

Think About It

Read a classic version of *Little Red Riding Hood*. Now look at the Big Bad Wolf's version of the story. List some things that happened in the classic version that didn't happen in Wolf's version. Then list some things that happened in Wolf's version that didn't happen in the classic. How are the two versions different?

If it had been apple season, do you think Wolf would've eaten Little Red and her grandma? Why or why not?

The classic version of *Little Red Riding Hood* is told from an invisible narrator's point of view. But Wolf's story is from his point of view. Which point of view do you think is more truthful?

How would other fairy tales change if they were told from another point of view? For example, how would Cinderella's story change if one of her stepsisters told it? What if the baby bear in *Goldilocks and the Three Bears* told that story? Write your own version of a classic fairy tale from a new point of view.

✦❦❦❦✦

Glossary

character—a person, animal, or creature in a story

narrator—a person who tells a story

point of view—a way of looking at something

version—an account of something from a certain point of view

23

Read More

Daly, Niki. *Pretty Salma: A Little Red Riding Hood Story from Africa.* New York: Clarion, 2007.

Forward, Toby. *The Wolf's Story: What Really Happened to Little Red Riding Hood.* Cambridge, Mass.: Candlewick, 2005.

Pinkney, Jerry. *Little Red Riding Hood.* New York: Little, Brown, 2007.

Internet Sites

FactHound offers a safe, fun way to find Internet sites related to this book. All of the sites on FactHound have been researched by our staff.

Here's all you do:

Visit *www.facthound.com*

Type in this code: 9781404866737

Look for all the books in the series:

Believe Me, Goldilocks Rocks!
Honestly, Red Riding Hood Was Rotten!
Seriously, Cinderella Is SO Annoying!
Trust Me, Jack's Beanstalk Stinks!

Super-cool stuff! Check out projects, games and lots more at **www.capstonekids.com**